THE MINIATURE BOOK OF
Gift Wrapping

CRESCENT BOOKS
New York

© Salamander Books Ltd., 1990
129-137 York Way, London N7 9LG, United Kingdom

This 1990 edition published by Crescent Books, distributed
by Outlet Book Company, Inc., a Random House Company,
225 Park Avenue South, New York, New York 10003

ISBN 0-517-03714-9

Printed and bound in Singapore

8765432

CREDITS

PROJECTS BY: *Rosalind Burdett*

EDITED BY: *Jilly Glassborow*

PHOTOGRAPHY BY: *Steve Tanner*

DESIGN AND ARTWORK BY: *Pauline Bayne*

TYPESET BY: *SX Composing Ltd.*

COLOR SEPARATION BY: *Chroma Graphics (Overseas) Pte. Ltd.*

Printed in Singapore by Star Standard Industries Pte.-Ltd.

Contents

Ribbon Rosette

NO ONE COULD DISTINGUISH
THIS ROSETTE FROM A
SHOP-BOUGHT ONE

1 Use gift wrap ribbon which sticks to itself when moistened for this design. Make a small loop by wrapping the ribbon round your thumb; moisten the ribbon and fix the loop in place. Now twist the ribbon back on itself to form a pointed loop, as shown; stick it in position.

2 Go on looping the ribbon in twists, spacing them evenly as you go. It is fairly fiddly but keep trying – you'll soon master the technique. You'll probably need to wait a minute between each fixing for the ribbon's glue to dry before turning the next loop.

3 Continue winding outwards in a circle until the bow is as big as you want; cut off the ribbon, leaving a small tail just visible. Attach the rosette to the present with double-sided tape.

Twisted Trim

TOP TALL GIFTS WITH THIS
DELIGHTFUL AND EASILY
MADE DECORATION

10

1 This trimming can be made to match or contrast with the wrapping. You will neeed the type of gift wrap ribbon which sticks to itself when dampened; choose whatever colours you like. The smallest strip of ribbon measures about 8in (20cm); cut it out and twist it into the shape of a figure '8'.

2 Twist the ribbon shape to form a point at each end as shown, then secure it in position by dampening the tape. Cut the next strip, about 3in (7.5cm) bigger; repeat the process. Put the smaller shape on top and in the centre of the new shape; fix it in place.

3 Make four other figures-of-eight, cutting each one about 3in (7.5cm) longer than the last. Pile them all up and fix them together in the centre. Put the decoration on your gift and attach it by wrapping ribbon round it and the parcel. Finally, arrange it so that each loop is raised above the others and not overlapping as they're inclined to do!

Ribbon Ringlets

SMOTHER YOUR GIFT IN A
CASCADE OF COLOURFUL
CURLING RINGLETS

1 Choose three colours of narrow ribbon which co-ordinate with your gift wrap. Using one ribbon, tie it around your parcel in the usual way, crossing it underneath the parcel and knotting it tightly on top; leave long ends. Tie a length of different coloured ribbon to the centre point, then do the same with a third colour.

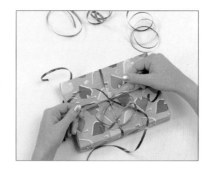

2 Continue tying on lengths of ribbon so that you end up with two lengths, (that is, four ends) of each colour. Tie the central knots tightly to keep them as small as possible. Pull a ribbon length gently along the open blade of a pair of scissors; this will cause it to curl into ringlets. Repeat with each length until they are as curly as you want.

3 An alternative is to use wide gift ribbon. Tie it round the parcel once, making sure that the knot is as neat as possible and leaving long ends. Cut two small nicks in the ribbon, dividing it evenly into three; pull it to split the ribbon up to the knot. Run each of these lengths along the blade of a pair of scissors until they form ringlets.

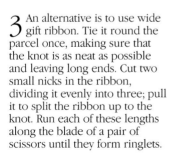

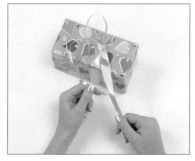

Floppy Bow

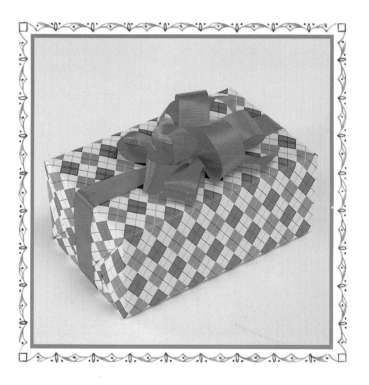

A SOFT FLOPPY BOW GIVES
A DELIGHTFUL FINISH TO
YOUR GIFT WRAP

1 You'll need about 6ft (2m) of acetate or craft ribbon, 1in (2.5cm) wide, for the bow. Cut off about 12in (30cm) of ribbon; wind the rest round your fingers. Holding the ribbon firmly, make a notch in both edges with a pair of scissors as shown, cutting through all the layers of ribbon.

2 Take the ribbon off your hand and notch the edges of the opposite side of the loops. Flatten the loops so that the notches match in the centre and loops are formed either side. Take the 12in (30cm) length of ribbon and tie it tightly around the notches as shown.

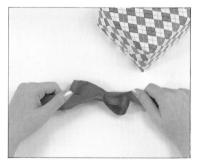

3 Starting with the innermost loop on one side of the folded bow, gently pull each loop away from the other loops and into the centre of the bow. You'll end up with each loop being visible, thus forming the shape of the finished rosette.

15

Delicate Doilies

THE DELICATE SILHOUETTE
OF DOILIES MAKES A
DAINTY FEATURE

1 Wrap your present up in plain paper and glue the doilies on to the sides. Alternatively, to decorate the corners of a large gift, fold a doily in half, then in half again.

2 Unfold the doily carefully and spread it out. Cut off one of the quarters of the doily; the folds along which you should cut will be clearly visible.

3 Paste the doily over one corner of the gift as shown. Repeat with alternate corners, unless your gift has enough space to take a doily over each corner without overlap. The doilies don't have to be white: silver or gold is also effective. Nor do they have to be circular – square ones would be smart on a square-sided present.

Frothy Frill

FROTHY NET AND A TOUCH
OF GLITTER MAKES A
GLAMOROUS GIFT

1 Cut a strip of net long enough to wrap twice around the perimeter of the gift, making its breadth about 6in (15cm) wider than the length of the parcel.

2 Gather the net in small pleats and wrap it around the middle of the parcel, as shown. Tie the net with narrow gift ribbon and leave the ends of the ribbon trailing. Gently pull apart the net tails. Cut another piece of net the same width as the first piece and twice the height of the existing 'frill'. Thread it underneath the frill and secure it with ribbon as before.

3 Put some silver glitter in a bowl and dab glue along the raw edges of the net. Dip the net into the glitter (this involves holding the parcel upside down). Shake off the excess glitter and allow the glue to dry. Curl up the trailing lengths of ribbon by pulling them against a scissor blade.

Fanfare

SIMPLE PAPER FANS PROVIDE
A STUNNING WAY TO
DECORATE GIFTS

1 Cut a strip of paper the width you'd like the fan to be when opened, and three times the length. Fold it in half widthways, then fold it up in small even pleats, starting with the folded end. Get a sharp crease along the pleats by running them firmly between your fingers.

2 When you have pleated the entire length, hold the pleats together with the folded edge of the strip on top. Bend the fan in half and stick the two folded edges together with sticky tape along their length as shown. Make sure the tape continues right to the outer edge so that the join cannot be seen when the fan is open.

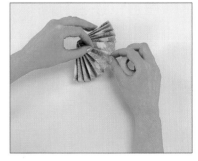

3 Open out the fan and apply double-sided tape to its flat side; stick the fan in position on your gift. Care is needed in deciding how big to make the fan – too big and the present will be swamped, too small and it will look insignificant. You can experiment with fans cut from newspaper first, to get the scale right before cutting your gift wrap.

21

Golden Gift

ADD THE FINISHING TOUCH
TO YOUR FESTIVE GIFT
WITH GOLDEN BELLS

1 Make two paper templates, both bell-shaped, with one showing the outline of the clapper from the bottom edge. From thin cardboard, cut out two of each shape.

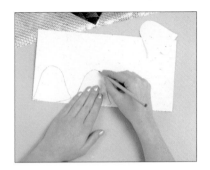

2 Cover all the cardboard shapes with gold paper. Cover both sides, and trim away all the excess paper. On the bell shapes with the clapper, cut a slit from the curved top of the bell to the centre of the bell. On the others (the plain ones) cut a slit from the middle of the bottom edge, also to the centre.

3 Pierce a hole in the top of the plain bell shapes and thread them with a length of ribbon. Then slot the pairs of bell shapes together (i.e. the plain one, and the one with the clapper) so that they form three-dimensional shapes, as shown here. Tie a group of as many bells as you like on to your gift.

Christmas Leaves

HOLLY LEAVES MAKE THE
PERFECT DECORATION
FOR A FESTIVE GIFT

1 First measure the length of the diagonal across the top of your parcel. Then, on a sheet of plain paper, draw a large holly leaf, the 'vein' of which measures slightly more than half the length of the diagonal.

2 Trace four holly leaves on to some green cardboard, using the template you have just created. Cut the leaves out and bend them in the middle, creasing them slightly where the central vein would be.

3 Make the berries from a ball of cotton wool wrapped in two squares of red tissue paper. Put a dab of glue inside and twist up the tissue tightly at the base. When the glue is dry, cut off as much excess of the twist as possible. Group the leaves and berries on the parcel and attach with glue or double-sided tape.

Fun Fold-Out

USE YOUR GIFT WRAP TO
MAKE CO-ORDINATED
GIFT TAGS

1 Select a gift wrap design that has a fairly large repeat. One motif must have sufficient space around it so that it can be cut out without including any others. Draw a rectangle around the motif, ensuring that all the corners are right angles.

2 Cut the rectangle out with a craft knife. Next, cut out a piece of thin cardboard the same height as the chosen motif and exactly three times its width. Fold the cardboard in three widthways, creasing the folds well, then fold the top two sections back on themselves, as shown. Mark the folds in pencil first to be sure they are straight.

3 Cut the gift wrap motif precisely in half. Glue each half on to the top two sections of the folded card. They should fit exactly, but if necessary trim the top and bottom to form a straight edge. Try matching the colours of the lining cardboard with the gift wrap; in the example shown here, red or even black could have been used for a different effect.

Name Dropping

MAKE FUN TAGS OUT OF
THE RECIPIENT'S NAME
OR INITIAL

1 You can either make the tag out of the initial or – even better – the whole name of the recipient. First draw the shape of the letters you want on to a piece of tracing paper. Make sure that the letters in a name interlock sufficiently.

2 When you're happy with the result, trace the letters (or single initial) on to coloured cardboard, pressing hard to make a clear outline. Use a ruler where there are straight sections to a letter.

3 Next, cut out the shape using a craft knife, carefully following the traced lines. Punch a hole in a position where the weight of the tag will make it hang well on the gift.

Paint Paper

SPRAY STENCIL SOME PLAIN
PAPER TO ACHIEVE THIS
STYLISH GIFT WRAP

1 Choose some plain coloured paper for a base, and make your stencils from plain cardboard or paper. Cut the stencils into squares of two different sizes; alternatively you could use any kind of basic shape – stars, circles or whatever.

2 Lay some of the shapes in a random pattern across the plain paper, holding them in place with a spot of Plasticine or modelling clay. Cover the whole paper with paint spray. Use car paint or craft spray paint, but do carry it out in a well-ventilated room.

3 Once the paint is dry take off the sprayed squares and put a new random pattern of fresh squares across the paper. Overlap some of the original squares with the new ones to create interesting effects, then spray the entire sheet with a second colour of paint. Remove the squares and leave the wrapping paper to dry before using it.

What's in a Name?

PERSONALIZE THAT SPECIAL
GIFT IN A SIMPLE BUT
EFFECTIVE WAY

1 Choose a plain wrapping paper for this design, and three contrasting felt-tipped pens. Hold the pens together in a row and secure them with sticky tape. Before applying the tape, you must ensure the pens are level so that each pen writes with ease.

2 Write the recipient's name randomly across the page in a rounded, flamboyant style. You could vary the effect by grouping the pens in a cluster, rather than a row, or using four or even five pens. Another variation would be to write the name smaller in ordered columns, to give a striped effect.

3 When you've finished covering the paper with the name, continue the three-tone theme of the gift by tying it up with three ribbons which match the colours of the pens. No one could mistake who this present is for!

Bags of Goodies

GIFT BAGS MAKE ATTRACTIVE
CONTAINERS AND CAN BE
MADE ANY SIZE

1 Find something with the required dimensions of the finished bag to serve as a mould – a pile of books should suffice. Choose a good quality, strong gift wrap for making the bag. Cut a strip of gift wrap long enough to wrap around the 'mould' and fold over the top edge.

2 Wrap the paper around the mould; glue or use double-sided tape to join the seam at the back. Fold over the end flaps in the usual way of wrapping any parcel to make the base of the bag and be sure to attach sufficient tape to make the base strong.

3 Slip the mould out. Fold in the sides of the bag, creasing them in half at the top; fold the base up over the back of the bag. Punch two holes, spaced apart, at the top of the front and back of the bag as shown. Thread through a length of cord to form a handle; knot each end inside the bag. Repeat on the other side. Alternatively, you could thread the bag with ribbon.

Little Boxes

MAKE YOUR OWN GIFT BOX
FOR THAT EXTRA
SPECIAL GIFT

1 This method is best suited to a small box as the end result is not particularly strong. From thin cardboard, cut out a cross-shaped piece as shown, made up of four sides and a base, all the same size and all absolutely square. The lid will also be a square measuring ¼in (5mm) larger than the base, with sides about ¾in (15mm) deep.

2 Paste both shapes on to gift wrap and when dry cut off the gift wrap around the box and lid, leaving a small turning or flap around each edge. Fold in the flap on the left of each side of the box and glue it down as shown. Score along the edges of what will be the base, to form fold lines for the sides of the box.

3 Bend the sides upwards. Put glue on the patterned side of the flaps of gift wrap left unfolded on each side; stick these flaps inside the box to the adjacent sides as illustrated. Crease down the sides firmly and leave to dry. Finally, fold in and glue the top lip. Treat the lid in exactly the same way.

Put A Lid On It

THIS PRETTY CYLINDRICAL
BOX IS IDEAL FOR THAT
AWKWARD-SHAPED GIFT

1 Wrap a piece of thin cardboard around the gift to determine the measurement of the box. Cut out the cardboard, roll it up into a cylinder and stick down the edge with a length of tape. Draw and cut out a circular base, and a slightly larger circle for the lid. Attach the base with small bits of tape.

2 Cut a strip of cardboard slightly longer than the circumference of the box. To make the lid, stick the edge of the strip to the edge of the circle with tape. Next, glue some gift wrap on to the box, allowing an overlap each end. Tuck the overlap into the open end and secure. Fold the base overlap in a series of small triangles and stick to the base.

3 Draw a circle of gift wrap slightly smaller than the base. Cut it out and glue in position, hiding all the folds, and bits of tape. Cover the lid in the same way. If you like, you can punch two holes in each side of the container and thread through short lengths of decorative braid.

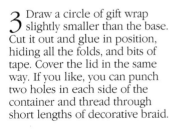

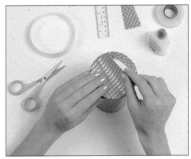

Buttons and Bows

MAKE A SMALL GIFT THAT
EXTRA BIT BIGGER WITH
THIS CLEVER DESIGN

1 Wrap the gift into a ball shape, then cut a strip of paper about three times the width of the gift and long enough to form loops on each side of it. Fold the edges over. Gather small pleats at each end, securing them with sticky tape. Pinch-pleat four gathers in the middle of the strip and secure.

2 For the trailing sections of the bow, cut a five-sided piece of paper as shown. Fold over the edges in to the centre at the back and secure with tape. Gather pinch pleats at one end and secure. At the other end cut out a V-shaped section to form a nicely-shaped tail. Repeat the procedure a second time.

3 Turn the pleated ends of the long strip to the middle to form the loops, and secure with double-sided tape. Stick the tails under the bow with more tape. Finally, put double-sided tape over the join on top of the bow and stick the gift in position. Puff out the loops so they look nice and full.

41

Soft Touch

DISGUISE THE SHAPE OF A
RECORD – MAKE IT LOOK
LIKE A CUSHION!

1 First create the paper tassels. Cut a piece of coloured paper into narrow strips leaving about 1in (2.5cm) at the bottom uncut so that you create a fringe. Roll up the fringe, catching in a short length of narrow ribbon. Secure the tassel with coloured tape.

2 Take some wrapping paper that is more than twice the size of the gift, fold it in half around the record and cut it so that it is just a little larger. Join two of the sides together with coloured tape along their full length, attaching the ends of the tassels at the corners as you do so. Put a strip of tape over the folded edge of the 'bag'.

3 Stuff the inside of the 'bag' on both sides of the record with shredded tissue, being careful to put some in the corners. Don't use too much or the wrapping paper will wrinkle. Seal along the remaining open edge with tape.

Hats Off

TRANSFORM A CIRCULAR
GIFT INTO A PRETTY
PINK BOATER

1 This idea obviously will only work on a gift that is circular and flat, so that the gift itself can form the crown. Cut a brim from a circle of thin cardboard and cover it with a circle of plain, pastel-coloured paper. Wrap the present by rolling it in matching paper, as shown.

2 Make sure the paper fits tightly around the base by folding it in a series of small triangles. Trim the turning on the top of the gift to leave a small edge; fold that in neat triangles too. Stick the triangles down on to each other with tape, making sure that the surface is left as flat as possible.

3 Place the gift in the centre of the brim and stick it in position with glue or double-sided tape. Cut another circle of wrapping paper slightly smaller than the diameter of the crown; glue it in place. Tie a ribbon around the junction of the crown and brim, leaving the ends trailing. Cut a 'V' in the ribbon ends and glue on a couple of artificial flowers.